THE EFFECTIVE
ENTREPRENEUR

THE EFFECTIVE ENTREPRENEUR

Fifty-nine Rules to Create Value Throughout the Life Cycle of Your Company

George Von Gehr

iUniverse, Inc.
New York Lincoln Shanghai

THE EFFECTIVE ENTREPRENEUR
Fifty-nine Rules to Create Value Throughout
the Life Cycle of Your Company

iUniverse books may be ordered through booksellers or by contacting:

iUniverse
2021 Pine Lake Road, Suite 100
Lincoln, NE 68512
www.iuniverse.com
1-800-Authors (1-800-288-4677)

ISBN: 978-0-595-41854-1 (pbk)
ISBN: 978-0-595-86199-6 (ebk)

Printed in the United States of America

CONTENTS |

CONTENTS II

Part 1: ACQUISITION STRATEGY

Part 2: BOARD OF DIRECTORS

Part 3: BUSINESS PLANNING AND STRAEGY

Part 4: COMMUNICATION

Part 5: ECONOMICS AND ENTERPRISE

Part 6: FINANCE AND FINANCING

Part 7: INTEGRITY AND EXCELLENCE

Part 8: INNOVATION

Part 9: LIQUIDITY AND VALUATION

Part 10: MANAGEMENT PROCESSES

Part 11: NEGOTIATION

Part 12: PEOPLE, ORGANIZATION, AND COMPENSATION

ACKNOWLEGEMENTS

Special heartfelt thanks to those who helped me write this book.

- For their editing assistance:
- Alice Acheson
- Laura Puckett
- Barbara Von Gehr
- For constructive comments and insights (in addition to those listed above):
- Sal Gutierrez
- Jim Kochman
- Rodney Perkins
- Allen Puckett
- Ed Michael Reggie
- Carol Sands
- Greg Von Gehr

And to our cats without whom I could never have maintained the discipline to complete *The Effective Entrepreneur*.

INTRODUCTION

THE LANDSCAPE FOR EMERGING COMPANIES has changed dramatically since the 2000–2002 economic downturn that washed out so many entrepreneurial endeavors. This book targets entrepreneurs, founders, senior executives, and service providers of early stage companies, who are seeking disruptively to change markets.

I have attempted here to weave a coherent fabric of the most important contemporary macro level principles. While many other writings talk about *how to do it, The Effective Entrepreneur* concentrates on *how to think about it.* I've included both time-tested principles and those newly honed from recent economic evolution.

These rules are distilled from my management experience with emerging companies, discussions with numerous entrepreneurs, and my career as an M&A banker for hundreds of young technology companies. In my extensive work with these emerging companies, I have noticed that the same questions surfaced again and again. The answers to these questions inspired and shaped my fifty-nine value building rules. At the same time, I also have had long relationships with and learned much from the venture capitalists, lawyers, and accountants who are the service providers that support the growth of these young companies. This resulting "handbook" provides a single, concise, encyclopedic resource for anyone involved with or interested in entrepreneurship.

The Effective Entrepreneur is organized around the life cycle of an emerging company in order to address major challenges through the following four stages of development:

- *Inception*—recognizing successful start-up alchemy; looking in the mirror for strengths, self-confidence, and leadership; developing business plans and models; leading innovation; and establishing a culture of excellence and integrity

- *Development*—selecting and organizing managers, teams and boards; creating strategy with vitality; building barriers to entry; and succeeding in negotiations

- *Growth*—managing through economic cycles with a global outlook; financing with debt, equity, or corporate partners; and understanding communications basics
- *Maturity*—supervising service providers; determining valuation as a function of timing; and formulating efficacious acquisition integration plans and realistic post acquisition commitments

Although these rules are sequenced according to the stages of a generic company's life cycle, the specifics of the company's personality, dynamics of its market, and available financing may affect the timing and degree of adoption of any given rule. For that reason, emerging companies may apply the teachings of different rules at different stages of their respective life cycles.

I intentionally chose a concise writing style that includes headings and bullets, a style that is direct and without excess verbiage. Two tables of contents, which list the Rules in different orders i.e. by chronology and by business subject, are included to increase the speed with which readers can locate subjects of interest.

Entrepreneurship is rarely described as fun. While there is excitement and great satisfaction in solving challenges that have little or no precedent and in being first to predict market trends, solutions are difficult to find and are extremely risky. The best answers are often found only by trial and error.

This book is dedicated to those who thrive on taking entrepreneurial risks and are searching for powerful yet thoughtful ideas to increase the value of their emerging entrepreneurial enterprises.

George Von Gehr

PART 1

INCEPTION

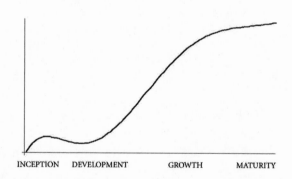

Rule No. 1

Starting a Company Is More Alchemy Than Analysis

THE FOUNDERS OF DELL, EBAY, AND MICROSOFT did not make their reputations or wealth by following a formula or by doing extensive research. Rather, their success is based on a fortuitous combination of:

- Entrepreneurial passion
- Intriguing market vision
- Strong product, market, and trend intuition
- Disruptive technology or innovation
- Effective communication of the vision
- Available resources, both human and financial

The combination is never precisely the same, even for serial entrepreneurs, but to some degree, the key ingredients are always present. Notwithstanding, sophisticated and successful investors instinctually recognize—almost as a gestalt—both fortuitous combinations of entrepreneurial ingredients and those entrepreneurs who intuitively and sequentially create successful ventures.

Charlie Palmer, a well-known New York City restaurateur (I heard speaking at the Gourmet Institute in October, 2004) admitted that his worst restaurant startup failure was the only one based on careful market research. Analysis cannot replace entrepreneurial intuition and passion.

Were you to speak with Arthur Rock, Tom Perkins, or the late Gene Kleiner, these famous venture capitalists would probably say that they looked for excellent entrepreneurs with companies possessing significant technologies that were, designed to change industries. I'm speaking here of companies like Acuson, Apple, Genentech, Intel, and Tandem Computers.

Related Rule No. 4: Business Plans

Lead from Strengths and Understand Weaknesses

EVERY ENTREPRENEUR SHARES SOME combination of the following often contradictory traits:

- Personal charm
- Frequent insensitivity to the feelings of others
- Short attention span—being easily distracted
- Capacity for intense focus and a sense of urgency
- Obsessive need to control the immediate environment
- Tendency to talk before listening
- Strong passion and intelligence
- Ability to make hair trigger decisions
- High tolerance for risk-taking

Entrepreneurs are mavericks and disrupters, a fact that often prevents others from supporting them in their ideas. These attributes may make them unsuitable for large companies; in fact, many of the most successful entrepreneurs have previously failed in those larger environments. (Rule No. 3)

It is old news that allowing others to participate in decision-making is critical for gaining support and achieving effective execution. But many natural entrepreneurial traits, such as impatience and sense of urgency, can interfere. However, if one tempers these traits, he/she can exchange them for group support and become the group's leader.

As Clint Eastwood, playing Dirty Harry in the film, *Magnum Force*, said, "you have to know your limitations." Another way to say this is: know what you don't know! In other words, get good counsel for your blind spots, and gather managers around you who are strong where you are weak and limited.

Frank Quattrone ignored Dirty Harry's advice, and the advice of his lawyers, as well, when he took the witness stand in his 2004/2005 trial (bibliography numbers: 14, 15, 16). The traits that had been important in making him the quintessentially successful technology investment banker were not well received by the jury. His conviction has been overturned and the Government has terminated their prosecution.

Related Rule No. 3: Exercise Leadership

Exercise Leadership; Believe in Yourself

FAINTHEARTED ENTREPRENEURS may lose corporate traction if they fail to:

- Display true passion
- Raise equity or debt financing
- Attract top management talent
- Convince major customers to switch to their products
- Withstand the many naysayers that routinely greet entrepreneurs

There are many systems and tests that claim to determine one's personal and management "styles." Whether you learn from these, from others around you—perhaps from family members or company personnel—or by introspection, you need to know a lot about yourself in order to become an effective leader. Successfully building an emerging company management team is the consummate test of leadership ability. You need to hire others who are strong enough to temper you, complement your skills, understand your weaknesses, and serve as a sounding board.

Strong leadership requires strong self-confidence. But there is a fine line between self-confidence and arrogance, and an entrepreneur must not cross that line. General Eisenhower, leader of the WW II allied forces, had to make extremely difficult decisions on the timing and location of the D-Day landings; he maintained the balance.

Entrepreneurs deal with so many constituencies that possess large egos—for example, venture capitalists or large companies—that there is little room for their own egos to intrude. Their egos must be strong enough to lead under difficult circumstances, but sufficiently controlled to listen to others' views carefully enough to consider changing positions if the arguments are compelling. In many cases, the carnage of web companies in 2000–2002 could have been avoided if those at the helm had listened to others. Use the ego for self-confidence but not for arrogance.

Martha Stewart, in her legal troubles, may have crossed the line into arrogance. To resolve her issues and keep them off the front page, she could have admitted her transgressions. But choosing to defend her actions, she became the focus of endless negative newspaper stories, *Saturday Night Live* spoofs, and criminal prosecution that resulted in jail time (bibliography number 15).

A good leader is to some degree a chameleon who adopts the appropriate style to fit the particular situation. For example, narrow-style leaders like Carly Fiorina, an entrepreneur, may excel in one environment (Lucent) and then fail miserably in another (Hewlett-Packard). Because she could not understand her "style" limitations, she was asked to leave HP (bibliography number 13).

There are three critical focuses for the entrepreneur CEO: product innovation (Rule No. 6), marketing, and sales (Rule No. 13). The first is the product foundation for the emerging company. The latter two are the windows to customers and the outside world.

Related Rules Nos. 6: Innovation; 13: Sales and Marketing

Rule No. 4

Business Plans Must Be Concise

A BUSINESS PLAN IS A SHORTHAND WAY to express a young company's positioning and its growth plan. The primary purpose of the document, however, is to create a meeting and an intelligent dialog with prospective investors and business partners. Above all else, this plan is neither a disclosure nor a due diligence document. Therefore brevity and clarity are the orders of the day. Due diligence will follow later, formulated by the investors/partners who ultimately become interested in the business.

Because of its ability to quickly communicate large amounts of complex information, PowerPoint—with a length of twenty-five slides, plus or minus five—is usually the format of choice today for presenting business plans. The first two to three pages of the presentation should make the following issues absolutely clear to prevent the audience from losing interest:

- Company positioning and market focus
- Differentiation factors
- Strengths
- Concepts behind the business model
- Barriers to entry including branding, intellectual property and know-how
- Composition of your management team
- Timeliness—why now? And market and technology rationale
- Financial and strategic needs

These first few pages, covering the subjects above, become an executive summary to use as a preliminary document for any audience, to gauge initial interest, and to fit with their investing or partnering criteria (bibliography number 5).

Caveat: to eliminate any unnecessary or risky disclosure, the material must be written as if it would land on your competitor's desk. Frequently the material does find its way into unfriendly hands.

Finally, it should be available to its audience without requiring a signed confidentiality agreement, which is at least a time consumer and may require further negotiation. As a practical matter of business efficiency, because they see so many plans, many larger companies and financial groups refuse to sign them. In any event, a sense of need for confidentiality is usually a sign of over-disclosure or paranoia, both of which are unattractive business characteristics.

Related Rule No. 5: Business Model

Rule No. 5

Business Model Tells Volumes About Management Competence

"BUSINESS MODEL" IS SHORTHAND for answers to several critical business development questions that will arise over a three-to five-year period:

- How does the business make money?
- How much money does the business make?
- How fast does the business grow?
- What are the financial risks for the company?
- How much capital does the business require?
- What forms of financing will the company use to achieve its goals?

Many managements show their business inexperience and naiveté by how they put this information together. Plans often show unattainable rates of growth and profitability. Questionable scenarios raise significant questions about the competence of management. The business model is, of course, only briefly summarized in the company's business plan.

Everyone knows that it is virtually impossible to predict the future of new products, technologies, and market penetration. But when trying to attract capital, refusing to forecast at all—or at least to make a well considered effort at forecasting—is not an option. Thus it is not accuracy but reasonableness within the contexts of the industry, product, and technology that are important.

What are the metrics of competitors from whom the entrepreneur wants to take market share? The glib answer is that the new company's products/technologies are unique and superior, and—to a point—this may be true, but reasonableness within the industry context is still imperative. The principal economic concerns are the cost and risk to customers when they switch to the new products and what the benefits of technical superiority will be.

It is often useful to cite similar or related startups to justify the proposed business model, but all too often these discussions degenerate into comparisons with Microsoft or Dell or similar high performers. Because there are few such companies, the comparisons hurt credibility rather than advance it.

The factors bulleted above are just as critical to management as they are to outside investors and partners. Management needs a business model that will sustain its hopes during the years of waiting for returns from privately held stock, and many new employees will have to be recruited based on these same plans. Unrealistic plans and financial models will make it hard to recruit outstanding people and easy to recruit poor ones. Your competence is revealed in the business model!

Related Rules No. 4: Business Plans

Rule No. 6

Entrepreneurs Are Usually Drivers for Company Innovation

SOMETIMES, THE ENTREPRENEUR is the creator of the inventions on which the company is based. More often, the entrepreneur is like the talented film director, Steven Spielberg, who may neither have written nor acted in a great movie. Nevertheless, he pulls together diverse assets to make a movie that reflects his personal insights and skills. Steve Jobs of Apple is a good example of entrepreneurial orchestration of innovation.

So in most cases, the entrepreneur may not be the inventor, technical leader, or best technology manager, but decisions on the development plan, product specifications, competitive intelligence, target market, and product launch should have the entrepreneur's fingerprints all over them. The recipes for time-to-market and product positioning are made from these ingredients.

Therefore, his insights and skills are necessary in reaching the critical objectives, which are to:

- Market a fiercely competitive product
- Create it by the most cost-effective process
- Achieve these objectives in the shortest amount of time

The CEO should be focused on all aspects of product conception, innovation, and development.

Related Rule No. 3: Exercise Leadership

Entrepreneurial Product Development Often Attracts Acquisition Interest

PRODUCT DEVELOPMENT IN ENTREPRENEURIAL COMPANIES is often faster, better, and cheaper than in larger companies due to the lack of overhead, burdensome procedures, fear of decision making, and bureaucracy. However, small companies, in their race to the market, often lack the thorough testing and documentation that larger companies can afford to offer in support of their customers. These trade offs may be justified in terms of time to market and overall development cost.

But acquirers often value this product development aspect of entrepreneurship. Many times they will acquire young companies in order to gain a combination of time to market and technological advantages over competitors.

To catch early favorable attention, products need to represent a significant advance over those currently available in the market. Small improvements or evolutionary changes rarely make the case for acquisition. In the 1970–1980s, Spectra-Physics, Incorporated's founder and CEO, Herb Dwight, expressly required that any product development investment required a "significant contribution" in product improvement as compared with other products on the market. Such investments, of course, must ultimately be defined by the context of the marketplace. Today this principle holds even more truth than then.

Avoid the "Enemies of Innovation"

BUSINESSWEEK IN AN April 24, 2006 article—"Become Innovators-in-Chief," (bibliography number 2) reported that, "Ideas are easy. The toughest obstacles, said our respondents, are developing speed and coordination." The following is their list of *enemies of innovation*—the percentage represents the respondents citing the issue:

- Lengthy development times (32 percent)
- Lack of coordination (28 percent)
- Risk-averse culture (26 percent)
- Limited customer insight (25 percent)
- Poor idea selection (21 percent)
- Inadequate measurement tools (21 percent)
- Dearth of ideas (18 percent)
- Marketing or communications failure (18 percent)

These factors underscore the importance of a properly designed entrepreneurial product development process. CEO involvement and focus should be designed to combat these enemies of innovation.

Related Rule No. 3: Exercise Leadership

Rule No. 9

Keep Capital Structure Simple

IN AN IDEAL WORLD, young companies would have only common stock and therefore simple capital structures. All shareholders would be treated equally regardless of whether they contributed cash or "sweat equity." This approach would require that boards and managements use considerable restraint in granting options, founders' shares, warrants, or other equity based incentives. As an alternative to policing the issuance of *common* stock, investors have gravitated toward *preferred* stock, a class of stock that gives cash investors first right to sale proceeds and various other protective and preferred rights, including special voting privileges.

Complicated capital structures cost money to track and maintain. Thus, each new financing requires a review of all the elements of the complicated capital structure, may delay the process, and often leads new investors to ask for more rights than previous investors were given. They ask these rights as a show of their strength in completing a difficult financing. Multiple classes of stock also cause investor and board tension and possibly confusion over which class receives proceeds in what order and which class has special voting rights. This class vote can, in fact, control some aspects of major decision making for the company.

Creativity can be wonderful in financing and often is the only way to raise money. Many venture capitalists love to brag about the clever financings they have done. But the more clever the financing, the more damage it may eventually do to the capital structure. Although the cash may arrive at the closing, the impact of the creative part of the financing may be felt for years and may ultimately make subsequent financings more expensive and difficult.

In an IPO (initial public offering), companies convert all stock classes to common just before the offering, and shareholders sink or swim together. In this situation, however, if there have been over-zealous grants of stock to company founders, insiders, board members, or consultants, the investment bankers will force the management side of the shareholdings into an "acceptable" framework. But it is relatively easy for the banker to do this ugly job when everyone is focused on the pot of gold at the end of the IPO's rainbow.

Integrity and Excellence Begin with the CEO

IF THE CEO DOESN'T LIVE, breathe, write, and talk about integrity and excellence, employees will not collectively and individually embrace these values. And if the CEO condones offensive behavior such as wild parties, harassment of any kind, frivolous spending, etc., then whatever mouthing he/she does about these values will appear insincere. The CEO must set universally high expectations and drive relentlessly to achieve them by example. Employees who don't support these values should be developed (trained), disciplined, or terminated.

Sarbanes-Oxley, revenue recognition rules, and MIS reporting systems are all designed to mandate accurate and timely financial reporting. They should be respected, but are only an expression of intent; integrity aspirations that will fail without appropriate CEO leadership. High standards of integrity and excellence result in hiring better people, attaining higher deal valuations, achieving more favorable financial performance, and creating stronger customer relations.

The case involving William Swanson, the CEO of Raytheon Corporation—a public company with eighty thousand employees—is an interesting example (bibliography number 10):

- Swanson authored a series of common sense rules, thirty-three in all, called, "Swanson's Unwritten Rules of Management."

- Raytheon published these rules as a small book and gave away three hundred thousand copies.

- Swanson eagerly took credit, writing, "… maybe you too can become a leader of a company, and maybe it won't take you as long as it took me to get there."

- On April 20, 2006, however, Cark Durrenberger, who read the book for which Swanson took credit, recognized that many of those rules—seventeen out of the thirty-three—came from a book written in 1944 by W. J. King, called, *The Unwritten Laws of Engineering*, which Durrenberger had posted on his blog.

- Although integrity is one of Raytheon's four core values, Swanson "laughed off the whole thing," saying that the book was free, and suggesting that there was no economic damage, thus missing the main point. In this, he coined a new rule, number 34, "… there are no original rules."
- He then blamed a staff member for this problem.
- It was only after the board reduced his bonuses and leveled his pay for several years that Swanson apologized.

Integrity is one of those things that, when abandoned, is difficult to recover. Due to the public outcry, the Raytheon board felt it had to do something, and so put a price on integrity in the range of approximately $1.50–$2.00 per book published. There are so many recent examples of lapses in integrity, such as those occurring with Adelphia, Enron, Radio-Shack, and all the stock option back dating inquiries. The results range from lost jobs and pension plans to possible civil and/or criminal prosecution.

PART 2

DEVELOPMENT

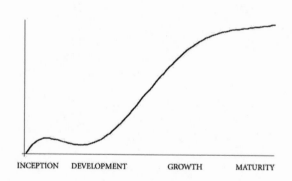

INCEPTION   DEVELOPMENT   GROWTH   MATURITY

Selection and Development of Managers—a Jigsaw Puzzle

EVERY COMPANY HAS A "PERSONALITY," a fairly direct reflection of its senior management style. As a result, each senior manager hired should fit together as a kind of six-part jigsaw puzzle. These are the pieces that comprise the successful manager:

- Specific job skills for the position
- Relevant experience and mentoring ability
- Personal chemistry with the CEO
- Strengths in the areas of the CEO's weaknesses
- Ability to develop other managers
- Personality that reflects that of the company itself

With effective selection, the team will lead from strength in a relatively harmonious way, and the development and execution of plans will be comparatively easy. Careful selection is necessary since twenty-five to fifty per cent of hiring decisions are wrong (bibliography number 18).

Informal performance reviews should be held quarterly and formal reviews once a year. The focus should be on both achievement of previously established objectives and job requirements. Communication should be a two-way experience between the supervisor and the subordinate in which the impact of the supervisor's behavior on the subordinate's job performance is discussed.

Most senior managers have a responsibility to mentor other managers in the company. For any employee in the company, the supervisor must chose between two options:

- Development of the employee pursuant to a specific development plan
- Terminate the person due to the lack of a satisfactory development path

Every employee should be the subject of a mutually agreed, one-page development plan kept in that person's personnel files. At least twice a year, there should be discussions about additional skills to be developed and specific actions required to achieve the plan's objectives. A development program may include reading books, program attendance, or other meritorious activity. At each review, progress on the development plan is revisited and the plan is revised appropriately. Mentoring and developing associates can be among the most satisfying experiences in business. They also dramatically improve performance, morale, and camaraderie. Consider also the approach of General Electric which uses an "ABC ranking" of its employees in which all "C" level employees (about ten percent of employees) were usually terminated.

Related Rule No. 12: Small Teams

Small, Strong Teams can Vanquish Large Armies

A SMALL, WELL ORGANIZED TEAM with clear objectives can always defeat a large, poorly organized or contentious army. In my opinion, the more senior the manager, the more time he/she should spend being proactive on human resources issues. The critical issues are motivation, development, and empowerment/engagement.

Environments that create high morale, motivated employees, and high productivity are the result of direct and clear communications, suitable compensation, and respectful treatment. Morale is highest in non-political environments. Internal politics reflect lack of transparency, secrecy, indirect communications, and favoritism.

Staff empowerment refers to delegation and visibility—such things as presentations at board meetings, working in small teams to solve problems, or implementing programs outside the employee's normal sphere of influence—that is, in situations in which they impact important decisions and have a chance to expose their abilities to higher levels of management.

High rates of turnover attest to the weakness of the supervising manager. It's best to deal with this immediately, even if the solution is to terminate the senior manager. In bad or deteriorating situations, good people are the first to go.

A *BusinessWeek* article (bibliography number 6) entitled, "The Managerial Moment of Truth," speaks of the need to remove or improve poorly performing managers in order to motivate others, boost morale, and increase productivity. The article says that a true test of managers is whether they can deal effectively with under performing employees through managerial tough love and that if they cannot, they are not prepared for management and certainly not prepared for senior management positions. (See Rule No. 11 for development and termination issues).

If termination is necessary at a senior level, there are at least two concepts one needs to embrace:

- Use the fewest words to accomplish the task; this is not a social meeting.

- Discuss the termination and not much else; litigation or severance negotiations may result, and you could be compromising your company's position.

Related Rules Nos. 11: Selecting Managers; 16: Retention and Motivation

Sales and Marketing Are Your Company's Lifelines to the World

SALES AND MARKETING ARE CRUCIAL connections to the outside world and, therefore, of great importance to the entrepreneur/CEO. Sales connect to the customers, and marketing connects to the competitive and market contexts. These are two of the three key focuses for the entrepreneur/CEO (Rule No. 3).

These functions have legendary tensions between them and often with the rest of the company. The following is a table to aid in understanding and facilitating management of the differences:

Issue	Marketing	Sales
Dynamic:	Reflective Analysis	Aggressive Pursuit
Metrics:	Market Share/Margins	Orders/Margins
Time frame:	Lengthy	Quarterly, yearly
Tension:	Current Market vs. creating new segments	Customization/price/terms
CEO Role:	Price/performance product positioning	Establish process to find, track, develop, and close customers
CEO Intuition:	*High*—enter markets with disruptive technologies	*Low*—target customers; when/how to close

The tensions between these two disciplines come to a head in the CEOs office, and—hopefully—the representatives of the disciplines find harmony there. What makes this reconciliation difficult is that one party to the conflict may be the company's best sales person and the other, its leading market visionary. The CEO must balance these natural tensions and provide leadership in making the intuitive leaps necessary for early stage companies to define their unique market niches and to determine how to reach customers. A dangerous dynamic develops when the CEO takes control of these functions without allowing other managers to participate in the decision process and/or leaps to conclusions without enough team analysis.

Related Rule No. 3: Exercise Leadership

Organize to Focus on Customers and Markets

THERE ARE THREE GENERAL ORGANIZATION STRUCTURES: functional strategic business units, and divisions (subsidiaries). Hybrids of these are common. These structures vary by degree of:

- Resource control and sharing
- Cost-effectiveness
- Responsiveness to market/competitive changes
- Corporate communication speed
- Relationship to corporate goals

Most young companies begin life with a functional organization since they start with a few products focused on one or two markets. Decisions and performance conform to overall corporate goals. This structure is the most cost effective and simple. Communication, resource allocation, and decision making go through the CEO, so, in the face of competitive changes, responsiveness may be relatively slow.

As products, technologies, and markets begin to proliferate, a different structure is usually needed to maintain focus on diverse customers/markets. The functional organization may morph into strategic business units (SBUs), which consist of a general manager, a marketing team and an engineering team. This structure has reasonable market responsiveness, but is more costly than the functional structure since there are manager duplications for different markets. The structure, however, does not control resource allocation for assets such as sales and manufacturing. As a focused group, SBUs are less oriented toward corporate goals than toward the objectives of their business unit and have reasonably good communication links with the rest of the company.

As multiple markets and products grow, these business units absorb more resources and become freestanding businesses or divisions (subsidiaries are only *legally* different) within the corporate structure, reporting to other senior managers. In most cases, these divisions have their own fully integrated operations, but sometimes they still share sales and customer service resources. This is the most expensive structure and is most responsive to their markets and least oriented toward corporate goals. Communication is within the division, and corporate communication to other divisions is slower and more diffused because they are separate units.

Which structure is most appropriate at any given time, depends on the relative importance of the bulleted topics listed above. As markets grow, one structure transforms itself into the next, and creative approaches allowing high levels of responsiveness to customers and markets are very much the norm.

Make Staff Meetings Productive

STAFF MEETINGS OFTEN SUFFER from a lack of productivity because they:

- Are too frequent
- Last too long
- Are contentious instead of problem solving
- Lack consistent structure

Since immediate problems are addressed as they occur, staff meetings should be less frequent than most managers expect. One can experiment with the frequency, but weekly may be too often. Less frequent scheduling encourages attendance.

Fixed agendas help provide structure and may minimize argument. Most arguments result from company politics and/or narrow functional, business unit, or divisional views. To maximize productivity and efficiency, it is the CEO's responsibility to remove politics from these meetings and to foster cross-functional or cross-divisional cooperation (Rules Nos. 12 and 13).

Most emerging companies typically have more opportunities than people to support them, so setting priorities for the use of resources—human and other—is a frequent task at these meetings. In addition, it is imperative to establish who "owns" or is responsible for each major initiative resulting from the priority setting. Ownership facilitates tracking and results in the owner feeling responsibility.

These meetings should also be time-constrained so that attendees can plan their days. Such planning also encourages a crisp trip through the agenda. If special topics need longer treatment, then notice should be given.

An important periodic topic for this meeting is progress on both the annual operating budget and the longer-range strategic plan (Rules 19–23). It is critical to recognize inflection points for each of these plans. If it appears the operating plan cannot be met, then the causes for the shortfalls are essential discussion points and may require a longer, supplemental meeting. The strategic plan may not be a normal agenda topic at *all* meetings, but when market disruption of a technological or competitive nature occurs, this event should be explored.

Beware of unrealistic operating targets accompanied by overbearing pressure to reach them, especially when these targets and pressures have major effects on compensation. These sorts of plans were the seeds for an entire garden of fraudulent accounting and high bonus payments at Fannie May, Enron, Sunbeam, Tyco International, and many other companies.

Related Rules Nos. 12: Small Teams; 13: Sales and Marketing; 19–23: Strategy

Executive Compensation's Watchwords are Retention and Motivation

MANY SOURCES PROVIDE REFERENCE information on cash compensation at different organizational levels. When designing incentive compensation, the difficult issues for consideration swirl around these factors:

- Cash or stock
- Mechanism determining payout
- Payout timing
- Provisions for change of control

Any individual's incentive program must be consistent with those of the other members of the executive group; there must be "parity" or balance across the group based on responsibility, experience, performance requirements, and total payout. Compensation must be competitive but not excessive. Consider the $100 million plus programs of Grasso (NYSE), Quattrone (CSFB), and Nardelli (NYSE:HD). Litigation may often follow.

Designing cash incentives involves two timelines: twelve-month horizons that increase motivation and multiyear—usually three year—horizons that encourage retention. In either case, each executive's incentive program should have at least two parts to the payout. The first part must be designed around the executive's specific objectives—both qualitative and quantitative—of motivating achievement of individual targets. The second part should reflect corporate targets to foster teamwork and long-term retention.

Ordinary stock options vest over time and are assumed to be strong retention devices. They may represent a poor program for the company however, because the executive gains stock rights, regardless of the executive's performance. It may be useful to custom design options in such that they have a second vesting standard tied to long-term company performance goals and/or to the recipient's objectives. The recipient's benefits are received only with both the running of time and the achievement of specified targets. Also keep in mind that some employees value options more than others do (usually higher management levels), and so indiscriminate distribution throughout the company may make little sense.

Sales compensation is a much-debated area. The only caveat here is, whatever scheme is put in place, the sales people will push it to extreme limits. So evaluate the structure carefully and anticipate all outcomes. Place caps on unlimited payouts.

In acquisitions, company executives may be asked to negotiate and complete a transaction in which they receive little or nothing for their stock; by this I mean those acquisitions in which the consideration is less than the preferred liquidation preference. Under these conditions, the board should provide a motivational incentive—usually a percentage of the price paid to the shareholders—as a carve-out before shareholder distributions.

Board Selection and Care is a Unique CEO Venue

BOARD SELECTION SHOULD FOLLOW the guidelines in Rule No. 11 concerning selection of senior managers. But there are some additional considerations:

- Some board members will be acquired as a condition of investment in the company, so make the best choices from among those investors.

- For critical strategic issues, select board members with relevant skills.

- The chairman and CEO should attend the board meetings in their entirety, but no other company managers should be on the board; this keeps the board impartial.

- Service providers such as lawyers, bankers, accountants, etc. should not be on boards for reasons of potential conflicts; but they can be asked to attend meetings as needed, or they may work through a "business advisory" board.

- Boards should be small with odd numbers, though few votes will ever be counted.

The entrepreneur's personal expectations for board members must be made absolutely clear, and annual informal mutual reviews between the CEO and/or chairman and each board member should be held. The purpose of these discussions is to improve the effectiveness of the board.

Selection of board members is critically important for another reason: removal of a board member is often messy. The difficulty is that board membership is by no means a purely intellectual matter. Among other things, board membership flatters the ego, and losing that membership is a blow to one's self-esteem. For this reason, specific terms in years are often suggested. At Hewlett-Packard, a director, George Keyworth admitted leaking confidential board information to the media; he initially refused to resign from the board, but later did resign.

There are natural times for board changes. These times include major financings, IPO's, recaps, CEO change, etc. Independent board members should head the basic committees of compensation, audit, and nomination of new board members.

Compensation of the CEO and senior management, in all its many forms, must be carefully reviewed by the board, led by the head of the compensation committee using outside surveys to benchmark decisions. To see the peril of a rubber stamp, look at the legal imbroglio of the NYSE relative to former CEO Richard Grasso's $187.5 million compensation and termination agreement (bibliography number 11).

Compensation guidelines for boards of entrepreneurial companies:

- Board members should receive stock but no cash compensation until the company is large, public, and profitable.
- To align their interests with those of the rest of the shareholders, incentives for board members should be based on a predetermined stock program; major investors serving on the board should not need any further financial incentives.

Related Rule No. 11: Manager Selection

Rule No. 18

Structure Board Meetings

UNLESS THE BOARD MEETING SCHEDULE is mandated by investors, schedule board meetings with a frequency that reflects the pace of company activity. Since many board members make their major contributions through discussions *out*side of board meetings, a better approach may be less frequent meetings—meetings held quarterly or semiannually—supplemented by status updates every four to six weeks via conference calls. The board must be nimble so that conference calls and meetings can be scheduled easily as needed.

To preserve optimal focus and maximize contributions of the board members, the meetings themselves should rarely exceed two to four hours. Materials should be sent out ahead by e-mail, especially indicating what decisions are to be made at the meeting and what the overall agenda will be. This approach allows board members to prepare and to ask for additional information in advance; hopefully this will result in more effective decision-making at the meeting. Board members expect regular updates showing progress and major decision points in the macro issues under consideration.

Presentations at board meetings should be made by a variety of company managers, in order for the board to become familiar with a broad cross-section of management. A major problem is that managers' presentations often vastly exceed their allotted time; one way to conserve the schedule is to limit the number of PowerPoint slides presented.

Some board members occasionally argue vehemently, over-focus on unimportant issues, miss meetings, or disturb the board's concentration by taking phone calls. Action needs to be taken to correct counterproductive conduct. The chairman or another board member must take the lead to preserve the CEOs neutral stance. The issues under contention must either be resolved, the board member persuaded to behave differently or be removed altogether.

Most companies keep brief minutes of these meetings. What is important, though, is to document, in the minutes, the basis for major decisions such as stock option pricing, senior management compensation, and financing.

Be Aware of the Company's Current Strategic Position

TO UNDERSTAND THE CURRENT STRATEGIC POSITION of an emerging company, several basic questions must be considered:

- Which competitive companies/products will be displaced to gain market share?

- Is the company just a product line or can it be a broader company?

- What time frame is required to increase the value of the company?

- How much financing is required to take the company to the next two or three levels of value?

- What is the realistic amount of financing available to the company?

A critical analysis is required to compare the company's product differentiation, cost/benefits, and performance with those of competitors; this work helps those involved to understand the realistic market share penetration, given the market dynamics. The conclusion reached through this analysis determines potential product line breadth and strategic viability.

If the company consists of a narrow product line, then the only strategic question is this: given a realistic level of financing, what must be accomplished to maximize the value of a relatively near term sale? Alternatively, consideration can be given to whether there will be enough financing, management capability, and product ideas to build a broader company.

Product line companies are often acquired by large industry factors. They are sold relatively early in their lives, prior to creating a large infrastructure, and do not make good IPO's. The highest value always goes to the first industry acquisition of a given product or technology; by the third or fourth deal for the same technology, the value of the acquired company is substantially diminished because of its reduced strategic value. During the 1990s M&A (merger and acquisition) craze, one could actually graph the fall-off in acquisition values—for example, for networking technologies—as multiple buyers bought similar capabilities.

A good example of building a broadly based company from a product line company exists in the form of the WD-40 Co., (NASDAQ: WDFC). When Garry Ridge became CEO in 1997, he decided to change the company from a one trick pony into a stable. Now, ten years later, after acquiring a number of other brands, he has added approximately $150 million in sales, roughly doubling revenues and greatly increasing the value of the company (bibliography number 3).

Management needs to be realistic about the amount of financing they are likely to attract, because that estimate will determine the time line on which the company is to be built. It may also affect the timeline for a sale, or be the incentive for undertaking an IPO. Given the knowledge of transaction timing, the range of transaction values also can be estimated. If financing is available, greater value is always accorded to broadly based, technologically related growth companies.

Strategy Is the Stream of Decisions and Agile Action

IN SPITE OF WRITTEN PRESS RELEASES, annual report statements, mission statements, etc., a company's business strategy is, in fact, the sum of management decisions and resulting actions. While some companies have high transparency so its actions and writings can be compared with others; many do not. While it is more difficult to determine the quality of the strategy of a private company, here are some questions one can ask in order to evaluate the strategies of those that are public:

- Where is the cash being generated and where is it being deployed?
- Based on press releases, annual reports, and 8 and 10K's, what are the significant management actions?
- Do publicly announced hires or layoffs tell anything about the company's plans?
- What are its financial trends, such as margins, earnings, cash flow, revenues, capital structure, and market share?

An illuminating example is Hastings Entertainment, Inc., (NASDAQ: HAST). HAST is an entrepreneurial company that is thriving in a business segment where Tower Records—who filed for bankruptcy—and Borders are failing. HAST has 154 stores in twenty states and trailing twelve months revenues of about $546 million, making it a small entrepreneurial company compared to its competitors!

What makes the company interesting is the very transparent way its strategy, financials, and actions can be tracked. The industry requires rapid changes as media trends emerge and disappear, experimentation in order to continue to offer new experiences to the shopper, and quick efforts to capitalize on those experiments that succeed while they are "hot."

The first thing one notices is their branding statement, "Discover Your Entertainment." The stores are positioned as an ever changing and up-to-date entertainment center. When a trend becomes apparent, they capitalize on it by offering unique services; they will buy, sell, trade, or rent books, CDs, video games, and DVDs. The store becomes a destination where one may go to learn what is new, to trade in old items, and to acquire the newest ones.

Its *Annual Report* has a banner that says, "Anticipate, Act, and Adjust;" a classic case of asking for ideas, experimentation, and rapid implementation from employees. Its strategy is agility in a rapidly changing world. The new definition of strategy becomes: forecast trends, estimate their impact, take action and experiment, and then frequently adjust the actions based on results.

Whether for large companies like Airbus, Nissan, or General Motors, or for your emerging entrepreneurial company, agility—which may be defined as the ability to see trends, experiment, and make adjustments quickly within the industry's time frames—is both necessary and critical in today's world.

Strategic Plans Result From Process

AN EFFECTIVE STRATEGIC PLAN has to be realistic, achievable, and should result from a process created and managed by senior management, involving as many employees as possible. Numerous books describe these processes, which usually consist of the following:

- *Inward facing analyses*: describe the company's strengths and weaknesses, especially focusing on technologies, products, management, financial position, and financing prospects.

- *Outward facing analyses*: describe the competitors, markets, products, product price-performance and differentiation, apparent opportunities, and possible vulnerabilities.

It is the matching of the inward and outward analyses that defines the strategic plan. To make the plan realistic, the company may find it necessary to make changes to staff, products, and technologies, etc., or it may recognize that there is not a fit, and then move to sell the business. Processes that become too mechanical or have no follow-up are destined to fail.

The expression: "key success factors," was authored by McKinsey & Company, Inc. many years ago. Those key success factors are the three to five most important strategic considerations that apply to a specific company, its products, and its target market segments. These success factors should be a major focus in any planning process.

The plan should:

- Be written; the briefer the better
- Offer clear mission, vision, or positioning statements
- Set forth objectives with metrics and time schedules assigned in order to allow its progress to be tracked
- Contain a statement of key success factors

- Make the ownership of managers' roles and objectives understood broadly within the company
- Be updated every six months or when a major industry discontinuity occurs

A long-range budget should be part of the resulting plan, but the budget itself is not the complete plan. Changes over time in the income statements, balance sheets, and cash flows have to be accounted for by specific actions, together with assumptions based on industry and economic considerations.

The strategic plan and its success factors should be reviewed by senior management at least semi-annually (Rule. No 15). If these become unachievable, a new or revised plan must be constructed to incorporate the changes. Strategic plans cannot be frozen against the dynamic economic backdrop of the business world (Rules Nos. 37 and 38).

Related Rules Nos. 15: Staff Meetings; 37: Economic Cycles; 38: Economic Impacts

Financial Engineering Is Not a Business Strategy

IN EARLY 1945, ADOLPH HITLER, in an impassioned plea, asked his troops for one more major push against the allies to allow time for a massively destructive secret weapon to be completed. Hitler knew there was no secret weapon, but the request worked wonders for the morale of his generals and the troops; it was an illusory narcotic—much like some forms of financial engineering. Hitler repeated this request more than once before his suicide and the German surrender in 1945.

Financial engineering can be a similar narcotic that hides the company's true condition. The result of financial engineering is inflated earnings, concealed debt, and, possibly, improper financial reporting outside of SEC guidelines. Once a company has this monkey on its back, it is difficult to get it off. WorldCom, Enron, and others have amply demonstrated this problem for us.

As in the case of Enron, however, when the financial manipulations inflate earnings, conceal debt, backdate stock options, or alter public reporting, they become issues of integrity (Rule No. 10), SEC rule violations, and possibly criminal liability. Additionally, the commercial banks, accountants, investment banks, and lawyers who may have been complicit in those ill-fated corporate actions, are not faring well, as evidenced by the large settlement payments made by some of these groups.

If these highflying managers had considered the possibly lengthy jail sentences, they might have decided against participation in Enron's fraud. I suggest that you check out the movie, *The Smartest Guys in the Room* about Enron management. This sorry scenario is replayed in every downturn after the peak of an "irrationally exuberant" market.

But there are times when financial engineering may facilitate appropriate strategic actions such as acquisitions, debt additions, or other legitimate tactics. Under these constructive conditions, the more creativity, the better.

Related Rule No. 10: Integrity

Rule No. 23

Strategies Must Create Value

IT WOULD NOT SURPRISE ENTREPRENEURS or investors to learn that certain company characteristics create value based on:

- Strong intellectual property and/or branding
- Increasing market share in growth markets
- Well differentiated and interesting flow of products
- Monotonically rising and rapidly growing sales
- High gross and pretax margins
- Low capital intensity
- Simple capital structures
- Customers which hold industry normal percentages of a company's sales
- Lack of legal disputes
- Stable, effective management
- Well defined objectives, positioning, and plans
- History of achieving financial goals
- Reputation for excellence and integrity

Similarly, certain things *reduce* value:

- High management and employee turnover
- Shareholder, employee, or customer disputes or litigation
- Weak or challenged IP or branding
- Difficulty in gaining or holding market share
- Continuing product problems and/or poor market differentiation
- Poor financial results
- Supply problems or volatile supply costs

- Large capital requirements
- Complicated or "creative" capital structures
- Constantly changing and/or unachievable plans
- Disorganized records
- Inaccurate financial statements

Before embarking on any course of action during which these issues would be discovered by due diligence, try to correct or at least neutralize the value destroyers (Rule No. 54).

Conversely, lead from strength in touting the positive factors from the value creation list during any deal, financing, or hiring negotiations.

Related Rule No. 54: Liquidity Audits

Build Significant Barriers to Entry

THE REAL STRATEGY QUESTION is how to keep, protect, and increase market share. The best answer is, "Through building barriers to entry by competitors." These barriers come in several flavors:

- Branding
- Possession of intellectual property such as patents, trademarks, know-how and trade secrets
- Product price/performance design
- Financial resources

In their early years, most entrepreneurial companies do not have financial resources abundant enough to acquire and defend market share. So emerging companies are left to the first three items listed above. Innovative design and product cost can usually be matched by competitors, which means that in the long run, the only way to acquire true market share and protection is through the ownership of intellectual property and by branding.

Branding involves positive positioning and identification for the company and its products/services. Intellectual property consists of areas of protected rights (patents, trademarks, copyrights) or company-confidential abilities (know-how) in the company's products/services.

Over time, a company may change its investment focus to alternative barriers to entry; barriers are dynamic, not fixed. In some cases, a company which initially acquires market position through innovative product design will subsequently invest heavily in branding and intellectual property as it grows. Most young companies start developing intellectual property and then transition to building the brand.

The strength and validity of intellectual property is never actually known until it is tested through litigation. Litigation is both capricious in outcome and very expensive. For larger companies, the outcomes can be earth shattering. For example, Research in Motion (Blackberry—NASDAQ: RIMM) lost a patent suit to small patent litigation instigated by a "trolling" company, NTP, Inc., and had to pay approximately $612 million as a settlement. Patent litigation is viewed as a competitive weapon by some companies and a lottery ticket by others; as a young company owning valuable IP, be prepared to be tested.

The costs of pursuing these barriers can be considerable, especially pursuing broad international protection that the company hopes might become an asset in a liquidity event. Barriers can thus be viewed as investments, not just expenses. They require specific plans to assure their systematic development. Strong barriers to entry into a given market position also build revenue growth and profit margins.

Barriers to Entry May Be the Most Valuable Assets in a Liquidity Event

IN A SALE OR IPO, the most valuable assets may not be listed on the balance sheet: brands (such as Google and eBay) and intellectual property (such as patents or trademarks). But to create this value, these barriers to entry must receive consistent investment, have all documentation in order, and be free of litigation.

The value of these assets should be reflected in actual financial performance and projections showing strong revenue growth, increasing market share, and above-average gross and pretax margins. Without this kind of financial impact or prospects, these intangible assets would have little real value. There are many cases in which a portfolio of patents or brands had limited value because of poor market acceptance of related products. Thus it is the utilization and financial prospects for the intellectual property or branding that creates value, not just their existence.

These barriers to entry must be fiercely nourished, receive full investment, and reflect buoyant financial prospects, or they may lose much of their value in the market place and, consequently, at a liquidity event.

Metrics Are Vital Elements in Management and Company Evaluation

METRICS ARE THE COMMON LANGUAGE of business and management performance. They:

- Measure the progress and status of the business, including sales processes
- Describe the status and progress of specific projects
- Determine executive and incentive compensation

Many observers consider financial statements to be the only business metrics. Actually there are many other important metrics, including daily orders or sales, returns, spending on various projects, etc. Compared with monthly financials, some measurements are important because they are used daily or weekly to predict future business trends. Other numbers are important because they are not included in customary financial statements, but may alert managers to early signs of changing business conditions. Some data not usually part of standard financials but which might be useful to track include:

- Economic indicators (Rules Nos. 37 and 38)
- Key industry standard operating ratios
- Major company program indicators

Jack Welch, former CEO of General Electric, in a recent *BusinessWeek* article, (bibliography number 19) identified the three most important measures of a company's health: employee engagement, customer satisfaction, and cash flow. Managers can track cash flow, but cannot easily measure the other two elements. However, frequent subjective evaluations do have merit. Each company will have its unique measures that must be tracked to determine its current business health and operating trends.

An alternative way to view a business's health over the long term is reflected in two measurable parameters that show the firm's market and pricing power over time:

- Changes in market share
- Changes in gross margin

Expense levels are determined by management, so profit before tax is a less relevant but still important measure.

Knowing which metrics are most important to track at any point in time is one of the CEO's greatest responsibilities. With this knowledge, the CEO will be able to focus the management team and make effective performance related decisions. One of the vital roles of the CFO or CIO is to assist the CEO in this effort through prompt reporting of metrics.

Related Rules Nos. 36: Economic Cycles; 37: Economic Impact

Strong MIS Is a Core Element of Successful Companies

MANAGEMENT INFORMATION SYSTEMS use metrics to help track business progress and to provide clues about future trends. At any point in time, every business has five to ten critical metrics that measure success factors, progress toward objectives, and indicate the health of the business. These critical metrics may change over time.

Management's greatest need is "interpretive information," but many settle for large streams of data—i.e., pure numbers lacking clear interpretation. Interpretive information means numbers that are presented as trends relative to other measures. Interpretive formats include graphs, ratios, percentages, and so forth. The purpose is to provide both a clear status report and an early warning system for possible changes in trends of future business performance.

The information system is constructed through the following steps:

1. Outline the most critical senior management decisions on programs, goals, and budgets.

2. Determine what interpretive information is required for those decisions.

3. Establish the most likely timing of each decision.

4. Prepare the interpretive metrics on a timely basis and distribute them to the senior management team.

5. Assign the aggregation and preparation of this information to a specific manager.

The first page of an MIS package should have a multi-windowed format covering the key interpretive metrics. Less important interpretive metrics are on the next page. Finally, an appendix may contain standard financials and other basic data. The entire package may be produced monthly or quarterly, but the critical metrics may be tracked on a much more frequent basis, depending on the rhythm of the business.

Virtually Every Problem Has Been Solved Before

WHEN THE CEO/ENTREPRENEUR faces challenging problems, it is important to remember that most difficult problems have been solved previously. In light of this fact, the CEO should:

- Define the problem accurately and in detail.
- Outline avenues of solution.
- Talk through the options with management and the board.
- Find and talk with someone who has solved a similar problem before

Some managers spend too much time grappling with problems and not enough time searching for people who have already solved the problem. Managers who have wrestled with the same or similar problem can offer windows into alternative solutions and how they weighed them to reach their solution.

Check with your board members, investors, attorneys, accountants, consultants, and managers of other companies to find the person who has wrestled previously with this problem.

There Is Always a Creative Solution

IT IS NOT EASY TO FIND creative solutions for challenging problems—they are rarely obvious at first glance. Creative solutions:

- Meet all the necessary conditions while optimizing the results
- Sometimes arise in group problem-solving discussions
- Often require a flash of insight by the manager owning the problem

How does a manager achieve this flash of insight? Some managers need to sleep on a problem, but others gain insight by talking it over with other people. The critical points are:

- Find your method of gaining problem-solving insights.
- Seek clever solutions tirelessly.
- Know that a creative solution always exists!

Finding a creative solution inevitably takes time and often includes some amount of trial and error to sort out alternatives. Enough time may not always be available, but use what you have and don't rush the decision. Beware of the natural tendency to emotionally block certain avenues because they are uncomfortable, difficult, or distasteful.

Rule No. 30

Negotiation Posture Is Determined by the Next Best Alternative

WHETHER HIRING PERSONNEL or selling the company, your negotiating strength and position are determined by the nature of your next best alternative. In a sense, this establishes your minimum or maximum values for that negotiation. What is important, from a company management point of view, is to establish a satisfactory backup alternative and then to understand its worth in the context of the negotiation.

Contrary to conventional wisdom, negotiation is not necessarily a zero sum process. Knowing what things are most important to each party is a critical part of the artistry. Negotiators often seem to want everything—even things of little value to them—just to demonstrate their macho strength. Therefore making "trades" is an essential part of the process, permitting both sides to receive suitable value and to feel positive about the outcome.

For a negotiation to be effective, conferring in advance with your board and/or with internal management is necessary in order to gain their support for the outcome. A carefully constructed negotiating strategy also allows a measure of victory for the other party so there will be support for the deal on the other side as well.

Listening to and Reading People Are Fundamental to the Negotiation Process

THE BEST ADVICE FOR A CEO entering a room for an early phase of negotiations is, "Be quiet and listen before you talk." Listening allows you to learn what the other side is thinking or proposing. Listening means not only being attentive, but also remembering what is said by both sides. If, in the later discussions over documentation, you can say, "last week we discussed this point, and we said this and you said that," you may be able to avoid a complete re-negotiation of earlier points.

Reading people is not the exclusive purview of mediums and psychologists. It is the systematic process of understanding everything about the people you're negotiating with:

- Their clothes, habits, and office
- Their position relative to the other side
- Their strategy and motivation for the negotiation
- What the economics of this negotiation mean to them

Every negotiation is about the psychology, function, and context of those you are dealing with. If you can understand what the other side needs and wants from the negotiation, you can often map a pathway to an agreement. Whether you are negotiating a car purchase, nuclear disarmament, or the price of an IPO makes no difference. Unfortunately, diplomats and entrepreneurs often lose sight of these rules.

Time Is a Crucial Dimension of Negotiation

A TIMETABLE IS A CRUCIAL FACTOR in every negotiation. A timeline should be made an essential part of the deal. It should include dates for documentation drafts, due diligence, and closing, etc.

In general, moving quickly is the right answer for young companies. Part of the deal-making artistry is to create a "forcing function" or deadline, in order to cause the discussion to move along quickly. For example, an entrepreneur may state that if the deal is not closed by the time of a particular trade show so the companies can present a united front, the deal is dead. Other calendar events or the presence of an alternative deal may be equally important. Having a deadline on your side, however, which is not shared by the other side, may be a distinct disadvantage in your negotiations.

Sometimes, slowing things down may be a necessary strategy. It gives you time to pursue alternative deals, or it may make those on the other side nervous so they become more likely to agree to your terms. Sometimes a slow pace is necessary to completing additional preparatory work for the negotiation or to perform due diligence.

It has often been said, "Every day a deal is not closed is a day it may never close." There are so many capricious reasons for larger companies to back out of high risk, small company transactions, that time itself becomes the entrepreneur's enemy.

The Secret Sauce of Negotiation Is Preparation

THE BIGGEST SINGLE FACTOR in effective negotiations is preparation. Preparation is the act of deliberately thinking about every issue and facet on both sides of the discussion. (Rule No. 31). In many cases, effective preparation means writing these things down or creating a notebook containing all the pertinent materials.

Undertaking this preparation puts the important information front of mind, where it will be accessible for the discussions. The negotiations carried out by those people who rely on sheer personality (as Vito Corleone, the godfather, might say, "Make him an offer he can't refuse") will usually not come out well.

- The following is a form that may be useful for negotiation preparation:

- Divide a letter-sized piece of paper into four columns: Issues, The Other Party's Position, Discussion, and Our Position. This format provides a row for each critical issue.

- Write the key points under "Our Position." This will help you persuade the other side that your position is workable and favorable.

You may or may not look at this material during the discussions, but thinking it through carefully beforehand allows you to be fully prepared on all points.

Negotiations progress through many stages. Some issues vigorously discussed at one point may be dropped later, so reacting calmly and letting the discussions take their course is necessary. This process allows one to sort out the real issues as the negotiations proceed.

Related Rule No. 31: Reading People

Know Where You Are on the Negotiating Power Curve

POWER IN A NEGOTIATION is a function of two factors:

- Merit (along many dimensions)
- Value of each side's next best alternative
- Location on the negotiating power curve

Which party has what degree of power in a negotiation can be represented by a graph of negotiating power. This graph may be imagined as a bell curve with the peak reached by an entrepreneurial company at the time of an agreement in principle. The entrepreneurial company's climb up the curve is based on which company made the initial approach, how much proof or due diligence was required, the results of the due diligence, the chemistry of the principal players in the negotiations, and the value of each side's next best alternative. Good negotiators intuitively understand where they are on that curve at all times.

Understanding your next best alternative and its value—Rule No. 30—determines one's willingness to compromise. If the next best alternative for a given party is unfavorable, their negotiating power tends to be weak.

A good example is the NFL draft in April of 2006, in which Reggie Bush, a running back from USC, was drafted # 2 instead of his expected # 1 position. In an interview on ESPN-TV, Reggie was asked how much money he lost by being drafted second instead of first. The essence of his answer was that this event will cost "some money but not too much." "Some" and "not too much" are, of course, not measurable, but the meaning was clear: Reggie slipped down the negotiating power curve by being selected second.

Once an agreement in principle is reached, whether the negotiation involves an acquisition, a corporate partnering deal, financing transaction, or product or technology venture, the power usually begins to shift to the larger company—or financial entity. As a consequence, the most important deal elements must be agreed upon then. This phenomenon is the reason that—when the entrepreneur's demands come late in the process—they are generally met with a resounding, no!

Related Rule No. 30: Negotiation Posture

Choose Your Medium and Your Messengers Deliberately

IN TODAY'S WORLD, two aspects of communication can be critical during negotiations:

- Media choice: as Marshall McLuan instructed us, different media have different impacts. In contemporary terms, the choices of media are: face-to-face meeting (with location being an important considera-tion), e-mail, phone, or PowerPoint.

- Who is doing the communicating: different individuals can be used strategically, when appropriate, to deliver certain messages.

In evaluating different media, consider how each will impact the course of the negotiation and whether that works to your advantage. For example, an e-mail allows a considered response, while the phone is real time and imposes the necessity of thinking very quickly. If you want to *change* a term in the deal, the phone is a cooler, more distant, medium than, for example, face-to-face meetings, and it favors the ability to say no without the taint of emotion. Whatever media you choose, remember that written presentations allow the more complex ideas to be communicated with greater clarity.

Different individuals can play distinct roles in negotiations depending on what is to be accomplished. For example, in a complex discussion, allowing a lawyer or CFO to formulate a potentially difficult written response puts distance between the entrepreneur/CEO and the communication. The fact that the entrepreneur/CEO didn't author the response relieves him/her of responsibility for any strong emotional reaction by the other party and allows him/her to calmly pursue the areas of agreement and those requiring further discussion.

The message here is: think ahead about the best media and the best per-sons to advance negotiation issues at each stage of a discussion. Ask yourself these questions:

- When is a face-to-face meeting required as contrasted to a different medium of communication?
- In order to achieve the desired result on a given issue at a given time, who should deliver the communication?

Some Generalized Negotiating Rules Apply

MANY BOOKS HAVE BEEN WRITTEN about negotiating skills, but it is worth noting a few basic rules that entrepreneurs often forget or simply overlook. Negotiation is indeed an art, but it is also a science, and these rules are part of that science. The artistry you must develop yourself or hire someone who has this expertise for these particular negotiations.

This art has certain basic elements. Here are some of them:

- Weigh the pros and cons of making the first proposal.
- Use short meeting time frames to force focused, productive discussions.
- Keep negotiations to a small group of relevant people.
- Make use of humor; it's a valuable tool.

A huge amount of nonsense has been written about whether it is best for you to make the first proposal. If you are trying to move the discussion forward, go ahead and make a proposal. In general, because there are many levels of approvals that are needed in order to make a proposal, larger companies are better editors than proposers. Each level in turn extracts an incremental "value haircut" from the proposal. Bottom line: you do not lose power by creating the proposal's skeleton. In fact, your doing so may help accelerate the discussion.

Faster, more effective negotiations may take place when you use the other person's analytical framework. So do your best to understand how they arrived at a valuation or an important numerical conclusion. You can lose hours arguing about the validity of alternative approaches, and often the large company's framework reflects what they need for their higher-level approvals. For example, if they talk about return on assets, don't respond with discounted cash flow. The decision whether or not to abandon your own framework in order to use theirs requires careful judgment.

Negotiations are most constructive when they come at the end of the allotted time. Meeting for two or three days is commendable, but the most productive discussions always take place in the last day or half day. Use short meeting time frames to force focused, productive discussions.

Work to keep negotiations to a small group of relevant people. The more people in the room, the slower and more irrelevant the discussion becomes. Each person not only wants a speaking part but also wants to make a "win" for his side. Therefore much time is spent in little "performances" instead of issue-by-issue discussion. Sometimes, it will be useful to form subgroups that meet briefly and focus on specific issues. Often the least "on the spot" authority may provide any team with a negotiating advantage.

Humor can play a wonderful role in negotiations. You can use it to break a stalemate, to diffuse tension, to relax the participants, or to show the irrelevancy of a contentious issue. However, if humor is not a natural part of the negotiator's personality, a critical discussion point may not be the time to start.

Related Rule No. 32: Time in Negotiations

PART 3

GROWTH

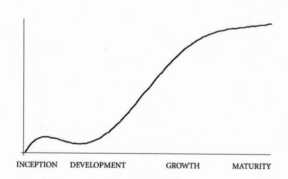

INCEPTION   DEVELOPMENT   GROWTH   MATURITY

Rule No. 37

Recognize and Manage Through Multiple Cycles

SEVERAL ECONOMIC CYCLES IMPACT BUSINESSES:

- US economic cycles discussed in Rule No. 38
- Global economic considerations discussed in Rules Nos. 39 and 40
- Industry cycles
- Financial cycles

Industry cycles relate primarily to what is in or out of favor relative to customer perceptions and financing opportunities. These influences arise from problems such as regulatory and safety issues or missteps by large companies that rub off on all the companies in that industry. The challenge for the entrepreneur is to reposition the company away from the negative whispers and squarely into more positive zones.

These industry cycles are the reason that private equity buyouts of public companies are in fashion today. With a public market looking ahead six to eighteen months, private equity firms can arbitrage these valuations by using a three-to five-year horizon to repair the business model and then sell or take the company public at a much higher valuation. A good example is the 2006 IPO of Burger King. It was taken private in 2002 in a large private equity buyout of a public company, and then taken public again four years later at a manifold higher valuation (NYSE: BKC).

Financial cycles also impact the availability and price of financing. The IPO window opens and closes over time for emerging companies and, at times, for certain industry groups such as biotech or energy companies. As this cycle rises and falls, so do the stock markets and the stock indices, which in turn determine the valuations of private companies for M&A and financing purposes. When a company prepares for a sale or IPO, comparing the transaction timing with the status of the financial cycle is a critical task (Rule No. 52).

Related Rules Nos. 38: Economic Impact; 39: Outsourcing; 40: Global Outlook; 52: Liquidity Timing

Rule No. 38

The Economy Impacts Every Company Every Day

CERTAIN ECONOMIC INDICATORS, domestic and global, affect every company. Senior management must determine which indicators most impinge on its company, and whether the business impact is a leading or lagging factor. These indicators should be tracked in graphic form and treated as important monthly inputs for business planning.

An example: in order to plan and maintain its strategy, a housing-related business, such as a home builder or appliance manufacturer, must watch and interpret housing starts, home sales, and interest rates. Of course it must watch other indicators as well, but these are especially crucial.

Good executives, instead of ignoring these cycles and dreaming that their company's progress will be forever upward, will manage their way through them. Since no one can control these economic factors, the skill is in learning how to navigate effectively through these phases in order to minimize possible negative effects.

Few imagined how severe the economic collapse in 2001–2002 would be. The first tangible sign was the April 1, 2000, public stock market sell-off. Effective economic cycle planning could have softened the impact on many companies.

Sometimes, when they are small, young companies have the opportunity to grow without interruption regardless of the economy. The day arrives, however, when they reach their equilibrium market share, making them just another member of that industry's milieu. At that point, management must begin to deal with the economic cycle impact.

Upturns and downturns have somewhat predictable impacts, especially for planning headcount or income statement projections. Every forecast must have an underlying set of economic assumptions. While the magnitude of the swing is not predictable, economic vigilance with appropriate planning will make the cycles less surprising and more manageable.

The moral of Rules Nos. 37 and 38 is that several dynamically changing cycles that are beyond the control of the entrepreneurs, must be considered in the company strategic planning processes.

Related Rule No. 37: Economic Cycles

Undertake Outsourcing With Eye on P&L

TIRED OF MAXIMS such as *think globally and act locally?* The question here is whether effective outsourcing is fact or fantasy for young companies. The conceptual appeal of the "virtual" company is great. Since little capital investment is required, and many normally fixed costs become variable, the belief is that outsourcing maximizes accomplishment while minimizing risk and cost.

There are some serious issues in outsourcing:

- Control of quality, specifications, and deadlines
- Mindshare of the outsourcer
- Protection of intellectual property and know-how (Rule No. 24)

But the very nature of entrepreneurial companies may marginalize the opportunity for savings that outsourcing promises. Here are some factors that enter in:

- Low product volume
- Rapidly changing products and technologies, resulting in short product runs
- Limited expertise if done offshore
- Insufficient headcount to support outsourcing.

Many emerging companies have successfully outsourced the production of product elements such as software or product subsystems. In any event, the company also has to maintain know-how and production facilities close to home, both for pilot runs of new or modified products and as backup for high demand. But don't make the mistake of imagining that managing *any degree of outsourcing* will be easy. Like any other important project, outsourcing requires intensive management effort.

In emerging companies, outsourcing solely for cost savings may be a poor strategy. If the product design can't command a premium value in the market, then the company will probably fail. Price competition is for mature companies with stable, high volume products, not for new market entrants.

Related Rules Nos. 24: Barriers to Entry; 40: Global Outlook

Emerging Companies Need a Global Outlook from Day One

GLOBALIZATION HAS THREE IMPORTANT meanings for the entrepreneur:

- Multiple market opportunities for product sales
- Cost triage—locations in which material and human cost factors are favorable
- The need for reconnaissance of offshore competitors

Globalization often makes it possible to find additional markets due to:

- Product differentiation and possibly higher market growth rates
- Currency values
- Alternative regulatory requirements
- Positive price/performance in competitive environments
- Government initiatives in the product market segment

Participating in global markets also provides the broadest possible window into competition. Important competitors often emerge in regions other than North America. Knowing of their existence and competing with them early is important from a long-term, strategic view.

While the presence of these factors may sound inviting, there can be significant costs that may offset the positive economics:

- Sales and maintenance support
- Tariffs, taxes, and shipping costs
- Business practice differences in terms of language and customs
- Requirements for local infrastructure
- Management of long-distance relationships

There are two additional considerations in a typically management-constrained entrepreneurial environment: first, whether the company has the management bandwidth to support the offshore activity, and second, whether it is a good fit with other strategic priorities. Many companies have failed in offshore markets due to resource collisions with more important priorities.

A constant issue when moving any product or sub-system offshore is how to protect intellectual property and know-how; in other words, how to prevent copying. There is no certain solution, so take reasonable precautions, talk with IP counsel, and continue to keep the heart of the product in-house or in the hands of a very close, trustworthy outsourcer. Learn from those who have done this successfully.

Related Rule No. 39: Outsourcing

Corporate Partnership May Be a Source of Cash and Strategic Assets

LARGE COMPANIES HAVE MANY assets they can provide emerging companies with:

- Financing
- Sales, manufacturing, or sales/distribution capabilities
- Product or technology development

Most emerging company corporate relationships begin with contacts into an appropriate operating division of the large company, and contemplate some form of strategic relationship involving business cooperation. Most large companies have fully-integrated worldwide operations which can benefit the emerging company. The large company's need for a continuous stream of innovative products and technologies is the glue that binds it to the emerging company. Efforts to reach agreement on a deal between the two, however, are often lengthy and painstaking.

Financing and investments are usually managed by the corporate office so that the relationship with the sponsoring operating division is only an introduction. The processes of presenting the company and subsequent due diligence are handled at the corporate level. The negotiations, therefore, are usually with two groups: the strategic operating group for the business agreement and the corporate group for financing.

Financing assistance for emerging companies can take the form of equity investment, debt guarantees, accelerated payment terms, or product development fees. While contracts are under negotiation, often the larger company will provide a cash advance or loan until the contract is signed.

In these transactions, there may arise some potentially sticky issues that require careful thought in order to reach an agreement:

- "Special rights" for equity investment or sale (Rule No. 42)
- Termination or exit provisions

- Intellectual property ownership and rights
- The hiring of each other's employees
- Access to customers and customer lists
- Pricing or payment terms for products
- Product service terms
- Allocation of sales resources for distribution deals

Related Rule No. 42: Partnering Courtship

Partnering Courtship and Divorce Is a Minefield

STRATEGIES MAY CALL FOR partnerships with other companies for any of the following reasons:

- Use of strategic assets such as sales channels, manufacturing, etc.
- Financial resources
- Beginning a relationship with a potential acquirer

There can be danger in early-stage disclosure. Due diligence must be carefully managed or the potential partner may:

- Learn technology and know-how which could lead to copying
- Acquire knowledge of plans for future products
- Meet key employees who could be hired away
- Become aware of critical financial parameters, such as when the money will run out

It is important to plan the split up or exit during the negotiation of the partnership when the parties are positive and relatively unemotional. If the separation procedure is not well defined, if and when the partnership does fail, it will be very difficult to negotiate, because at that time, emotions and blame will be rampant. Disney had two corporate "divorces" one with Miramax and the other with Pixar, both of which had to be negotiated while emotions and media attention were intense.

Also be aware that some would-be or actual partners may have deep pockets and an arsenal of "dirty tricks" such as IP litigation. They may also have PR firms on retainer to muddy the waters and damage the emerging company. A good example is the Paramount Studios termination of its relationship with Tom Cruise when its Chairman suggested Cruise had personality problems.

Larger companies work from the inherent advantages of financial resources and size. A broken deal in which both parties have invested much time and effort can be devastating to the smaller, emerging company, but have minimal impact on the other side.

The time-tested adage, "know with whom you are dealing" applies. And here is another important axiom: *the best indicator of the future is history*. Make sure to check your partner's history of litigation and emerging company deal-making techniques.

Related Rule No. 41: Corporate Partnerships

Raising Equity Is About Exclusivity and Scarcity

IF YOU ASK VENTURE CAPITALISTS about their most successful deals, many will tell stories of how they created a company and allowed only a few groups to invest; or they will tell about those times when they were lucky enough to get into a very limited, exclusive financing. Such stories are always about exclusivity— the opportunity was only available by invitation to a few chosen investors. These kinds of financings should be the objective of most emerging companies; they come together very quickly and are closed by the time most investors hear about them.

It is also important, if possible, to size the investment so it can be completed quickly by relatively few investors and therefore becomes "scarce."

The reverse side of these stories is that it becomes more difficult to raise money if:

- The investment opportunity is offered to large groups of investors
- A large amount of financing is required
- The contact list keeps expanding as discussions proceed
- Financing remains uncompleted for a "long" period of time and becomes "shopworn"

Time is always the enemy when financings remain open too long. The essence of the process is to find the "lead" investor behind which others will quickly follow. Sometimes investors who are already on board can provide that leadership. But if this "bell cow" does not emerge fairly quickly, the concepts of scarcity and exclusivity will be lost.

The loss of these elements means a reduced valuation and possibly fewer dollars for the company. When they finally do come into the financing, it also usually results in the company's having to offer increased investor rights as "sweeteners." When investors ask for warrants and other creative sweeteners, be mindful of future consequences (Rule No. 9).

Generally, since the presence of one large investor may allow that investor too much power, it is best to have at least two major investors to achieve board and influence balance.

One rule, however, is always true: if the company and CEO don't treat the company's stock as highly valuable, no one else ever will.

Related Rule No. 9: Capital Structure

Rule No. 44

Raise Cash While Minimizing Equity Dilution

NON-EQUITY CASH can be raised by:

- Liquidating assets
- Borrowing against assets or arranging unsecured credit
- Extending accounts payable

Most entrepreneurial companies are unfamiliar with the non-equity forms of financing regularly used by large companies. Such financing may buy the company time to complete another, larger equity financing, or to complete a sale.

The financial manager should review the list of assets to determine what could be sold or financed. Even a sale and leaseback of some assets such as real estate may buy crucial time for the company. Similarly, the financial manager should review liabilities with an eye to extending them or negotiating payment reduction (forbearance), both of which reduce cash outflow.

Emerging company debt-based financing is considered *high risk* to the lenders and, therefore, *high cost* to the borrowers, involving higher interest rates, blanket liens, and/or warrants. Other well-developed forms of emerging company debt financing also include warrants. These financing methods are typically a form of debt and therefore must be repaid, often on a monthly basis, but they can create time to complete other transactions.

The merit of any of these transactions depends on the merit of the next best financing alternative, the benefit of additional time, and the urgency of the cash need (Rule No. 30). The company's bankers, investors, attorneys, and board members are good sources of leads for firms offering these financing products.

Related Rule No. 30: Negotiation Posture

Communication Is At the Heart of the CEO Role

AN ENTREPRENEUR/CEO is often thrust onto center stage, which can be an ego gratifying experience, but not be free to say just anything. The rules of communication must be followed.

An effective CEO masters the basic skills of communication to achieve both information transfer and persuasion in all forms:

- Spoken
- Written prose (letter or e-mail)
- PowerPoint presentations

Many CEOs will not be comfortable in all these communication modes, and yet must be able to handle all of them effectively. The same rules apply whether the communication is internal (upward, lateral, or downward) or external.

At the same time, the communication must be appropriate for the audience. The CEO has multiple constituencies:

- Senior management and a board of directors
- Employees and their families
- Customers and suppliers
- Industry observers, competitors, etc.
- Trade and general media
- Financial community

Each constituency has different interests, perspectives, methods by which they acquire information, and things that they want to know. If the entrepreneur considers these factors before communicating, the likelihood of success increases.

In order to appreciate the importance of these communication rules, one only has to watch the evening news and observe the large number of speaking missteps public figures make (Rule No. 49).

Related Rule No. 49: Off the Record

Rule No. 46

Learn Communication Basics

THE FUNDAMENTAL watchwords are:

- Accessible
- Credible
- Direct

Ignoring these watchwords has led to the downfall or decreased influence of many politicians and corporate chiefs. Think of Al Gore, Pope Benedict, Jeff Skilling, and many others. Sometimes the greatest skill is to say nothing.

According to some experts, a large part of communication—sixty to seventy percent—is non-verbal body language. Be mindful of the message you are sending from your body positions as well as by your words (bibliography number 17).

Much of communication is about setting expectations. We live in a culture of over-hyping almost everything. Sometimes the smartest course is to follow the example of Lou Holtz, former head coach of Notre Dame's football team. When interviewed before the game, he would marvel that the Notre Dame team was even worthy of playing on the same field as the opponent. Then Notre Dame would often win handily.

When communication of any kind is necessary, understand message positioning (Rule No. 47) and the priority list of themes that need to be stressed. If the message is too complex, ranges through many scattered subjects, or doesn't reach a recognizable conclusion, the audience will become confused, or, worse yet, they will lose interest. Be clear and direct and know when you have said enough. Communications of any appreciable length should build to a crescendo leading to the final positioning statement and conclusion.

Companies often use advisers to help them with certain aspects of corporate communications. As in all things entrepreneurial, selection and management of these advisors is an important issue (Rule No. 50). The more vanilla, "cookie cutter," and "standard" the advisors' recommendations, the less useful the recommendations will be. As in so many areas of entrepreneurship, effective communication requires an understanding of the communications process, how to shape the message, and involves using imagination.

A logical question: how does one improve on communication skills? Again it is usually advisable to talk with people who do it well. There are many instructive courses and materials to read. Some public relations professionals can be helpful, but beware of too much "standard" advice—advice that won't fit the specific facts that now surround emerging companies.

Related Rules Nos. 47: Positioning; 50: Managing Advisors

Rule No. 47

Understand the Difference Between Facts and Positioning

EVERY COMMUNICATION SHOULD START with a positioning statement that covers what is going to be said and how the audience should think about it. The same principle applies to the conclusion of the communication.

Many company materials recite long lists of facts, but fail to establish in the minds of the readers the unusual factors about the company that are:

- Specific
- Differentiated
- Important

The message must distinguish your company's style from others, and be both forward and market looking, representing its future objectives. The entrepreneur's positioning job is to "write" the critical conclusions on the minds of the listeners, shaping what they actually understand from the communication.

Positioning is interpretation of the facts—some would call it "spin." Positioning provides interpretation of the facts exactly as you want your audience to see them. For business purposes, you cannot be happy with having painted an impressionistic picture that allows the viewer to reach just *any* conclusion. Instead, you must provide the precise interpretation which defines your business objectives for that given audience and communication and is validated by the facts as well.

Talking to the Financial Community Is an Acquired Skill

FOR PUBLIC COMPANIES, the rules for financial communication can be derived from a simple picture: imagine the desk of a financial analyst, money manager, or investment banker covered with press releases, business plans, and prospectuses. In the first few minutes of your conversation with this incredibly busy person, you must answer three basic, essential questions:

- Why specifically is my company uniquely interesting?
- Why should you spend time covering or working with my company?
- How will you make money from the relationship with my company?

These questions go directly to the subject of that financial industry person's earning power. If there is no basis for enhancing the other individual's earning power, don't waste his/her time with a conversation.

For private companies talking to members of the financial community (venture capitalists or bankers) about financing the entrepreneurial company, the questions are fairly similar:

- Why specifically is my company uniquely interesting?
- Why should you consider investing in or working with my company?
- How does my company fit your financing philosophy?

Remember, when seeking financing you can again imagine a desk piled high with business plans and your needing to get and retain that person's attention. You must make your plan leap to the top of the pile.

Any relationship with financial groups ultimately revolves around two factors: access and credibility. Access has to do with the company's being easily reachable on the phone or in person. Credibility flows from rapid follow-up on previous discussions and the reasonableness of your business plans and concepts. You will be tested often on the substance of these two words: *access* and *credibility*.

The medium through which both public and private companies communicate with the financial community is usually PowerPoint presentations. Consider this rule: the second slide and the final slide should be similar in that they should position the company in the viewers' minds (Rule No. 46).

Related Rules Nos.46: Communication Basics; 47: Positioning

Rule No. 49

There Is No Such Thing as "Off the Record"

ONCE INFORMATION IS GIVEN, it can never be retrieved, or to say it another way, as President Bush and Vice President Cheney have discovered, an open microphone lives forever. The "juicier" the material, the more difficult it is to control its repetition and dissemination.

There are many famous examples:

- Rev. Jesse Jackson's referral to New York as "Hymietown"—uttered in a private conversation but it quickly made its way into the national media
- Senator George Allen's "Macaca" statement at a private meeting caught on a home video camera and then quickly appeared on national news
- Mel Gibson's anti-Semitic rant during a DUI arrest; this was part of the police report and from there it rocketed into the national media

If apologies are to be issued, speed is essential. A slow apology keeps the controversy in the headlines and raises doubts about the speaker's sincerity.

- 86 -

PART 4

MATURITY

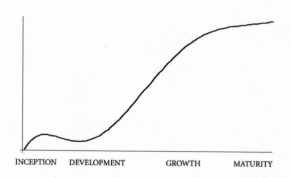

INCEPTION   DEVELOPMENT   GROWTH   MATURITY

External Professionals Must Be Actively Managed

STRANGE AS IT MAY SEEM, many senior executives are afraid to actively manage their professional service providers—by which I mean lawyers, investment bankers, accountants, consultants, etc. Given that they work for and are paid by the company, active management is necessary for the achievement of company objectives in the most cost-effective and timely manner.

When hiring these professionals, several things should be clarified:

- The role they are expected to play in the company—i.e., their duties
- Expectations for performance—i.e., their objectives
- What response times will be expected of them
- Who their company interface will be
- What kind of chemistry they are expected to have with company managers
- What expense levels they are expected to maintain

Selection of these professionals should result from interviews along the lines listed above and in Rule No. 11.

The ideal source for information about external professional services providers is previous experience with them. Recommendations from investors, board members, and other managers are useful, but require due diligence and should not be followed blindly. All professionals should be subject to semi-annual or annual performance reviews just as with senior managers (Rule No. 11).

One comment about budgets and expense levels: contrary to conventional wisdom, professionals can work to a budget. Don't be afraid to set expense levels; they usually dislike this limitation but will respect the company for imposing it.

Reasons to fire or not engage certain professionals:

- Client conflicts
- Inattention to the task or slow response times

- Reversals or incorrect professional advice
- Changes in the staff they your work to
- Poor attitude
- Grandstanding by providing unhelpful or lengthy opinions at board, management, or shareholder meetings—especially if these opinions have not been previously expressed to management

No matter which executive manages these relationships, that executive must report frequently to the senior team on service provider performance reviews, objectives, results and expenses.

Related Rule No. 11: Manager Selection

Rule No. 51

Know When to Pass the Baton

PRODUCTS, INDUSTRIES, AND ENTREPRENEUR/CEOs all have life cycles. Often a clear moment exists for an entrepreneur/CEO—especially if that person is the founder—to change roles, whether to lead R&D, become chairman, take only a board role, or to leave the company altogether. Such a change is based on the realization that the person's strengths are no longer the ones a CEO needs to develop the business.

It is rather common for a founder's relationship with the company to be likened to that of a parent and child. Good parenting of an emerging company requires both continuous and deep introspection. A role transition does not represent failure; quite the contrary, it can be the ultimate opportunity to lead. As Bill O'Reilly of Fox News might say, "a no ego, no spin zone."

When boards of directors find it necessary to remove the CEO, it is often very late relative to the need, and usually very disruptive to the company. But the CEO who takes the initiative and assists in the transition, will be admired for having made this move, will enhance company stature and boost its prospects for future success. And that isn't all. Such a CEO will be more likely to obtain investor support for personal future endeavors.

Some of the signs that the CEO has reached this career inflection point are:

- Poor results in aspects of the business managed by the entrepreneur
- Frequent management disagreements, especially on strategy
- Above average turnover
- Recurring impatience of board of directors

Bill Gates provides two good examples: first, when he brought in Steve Ballmer as president; and second, when he announced that in several years he would step back from management at Microsoft to focus on his philanthropic foundation.

Liquidity Timing Is a Major Determinant of Value

THE VALUATION OF A COMPANY at a given moment is strongly affected by four cycles:

- Economic cycles in the regions where the company is located and does business
- Cycles in the financial community's view of the company's industry
- Cycles of finance in the US and global markets—i.e., the status of M&A and public stock markets (Rules No. 37 and 38)
- Cycles in the status of the company's development

Maximum valuation is achieved when all four economic cycles are coincidentally high and strong, (e.g., 1997–2000 and 2005–2006). Many times these cycles are not precisely coincident, or there are events in the industry that so taint the company's value that the status of the other cycles is unimportant (Rules No. 37 and 38). Company valuation rises and falls with these cycles, as do public stocks.

There is no single formula for valuation, so deriving the ultimate valuation range remains highly subjective (Rule No. 53). But it is important to accept the absolute presence of these cycles and their impact on company valuation.

The business decision for an entrepreneur is whether to pursue a liquidity event at a time when the cycles are favorable but the company itself is not at peak value, or to allow the company to develop further (costing more cash and dilution as well as risk), and face the possibility of less auspicious cycles. Deciding to wait on company development trades off valuation, company performance, cash investment, and dilution, as the company strives for higher performance levels.

Between the pressure from investors to realize a high valuation and the banking firms' natural desire to please management, entrepreneurs must be thoughtful about the valuations presented by outside firms. To win the business, investment bankers seeking to engage the company for M&A or IPO may be deliberately over-optimistic in their valuation and timing assessments. For firms seeking to sign up clients, appropriate timing is usually close at hand, regardless of the external economic reality.

The best, but not infallible, approach is to triangulate through presentations by several firms. Or better still, to have a knowledgeable "friend" of the company analyze the valuation analyses and critical assumptions.

Related Rules Nos. 37: Economic Cycles; 38: Economic Impact; 53: Valuation

Rule No. 53

Valuation Analyses Are Subjective

ALTHOUGH APPEARING MATHEMATICAL, valuation analyses are more or less subjective depending on the assumptions, the nature of the "triangulation" methodology, and how the multiple results are averaged. Today, endless data is available; the issue is how to use it. In a typical analysis, several different methodologies are used to triangulate or confirm a company's valuation. These include looking at:

- Comparable public companies—i.e., in size, product, and technologies
- Similar completed transactions—i.e., in size, products, technologies, and type of deal consideration
- Discounted cash flow analyses
- Comparisons, if relevant, of private equity buyouts, venture capital financings, etc., for comparably situated companies

The first two and the fourth items above are generally backward looking and historically based in terms of valuation. The third methodology, discounted cash flow, is forward looking and that is why some combination or balancing (averaging) of these approaches is necessary.

Against this mosaic backdrop of analyses, buyers prefer valuations based on history, and sellers tend to view them in terms of future projections. It is the negotiation process that brings these different views together.

There are several guidelines for using these methodologies:

- Financial and economic assumptions must be clearly indicated.
- Populations of at least five similar companies must be used, not just one or two data points.
- Performance comparisons of the valued company with the sample set must make percentage adjustments for any differences.
- Adjustments are generally quite subjective since there is no standard mathematical formula.

- "Similar" companies can always be found.

There is also a concept of "strategic value," which consists of considering the benefits that accrue to a given business combination that neither company could achieve alone. Examples: greater customer revenues due to a larger sales force, reduced cost of goods, or reduced administrative costs. Many buyers feel the price of the deal entitles them to these benefits, but usually the seller can negotiate for some of them, which increases the deal price but lowers the buyer's ROI.

Because these approaches and assumptions can vary markedly, valuation should be generally expressed as a range, not a single number. In negotiations, of course, discussions center on specific numbers and not ranges.

Perform Liquidity Audits Annually

THE PURPOSE OF A LIQUIDITY AUDIT is to prepare a company for sale or IPO in the future. The process is designed to:

- Find issues that need to be fixed or changed in order to go successfully through due diligence.
- Consider the best timing, from a valuation perspective, for a transaction, as outlined in Rule No. 52.

The audit starts with a comprehensive due diligence list which most law firms or investment bankers can provide; this list consists of about thirty pages of questions. Typically, the financial manager goes through the list and then reports back to the senior management on what kinds of issues exist, and with a plan for resolving them. Some frequently cited examples are as follows:

- Contracts are incomplete, not up to date on terms, or not written. Examples of these might be facilities leases or distribution agreements.
- Board minutes are not up to date.
- Stock option grant papers are incomplete or inaccurate.
- Financial audits have footnotes calling for some action not yet taken.
- Employment records are incomplete.

There also may be other kinds of situations that require time to resolve; for example, management problems or streamlining the company. Such actions could include the following:

- Sale of a product line that is mature or sells to an unrelated market
- Sale of a product line to create a "pure play" technology in the rest of the company
- Restructuring of the board of directors
- Removal of a founder or other senior manager

By performing this audit, records can be brought up to date while there is ample time to correct any problems the audit may uncover. For example, the worst time to complete/correct a facility lease is when the landlord suspects a large buyer is in the wings. Another reason to keep this process up to date is that buyers often appear unexpectedly. As noted in Rule No. 33, preparation is the most important factor in a successful negotiation on company value. The more "in order" a company appears, the greater the chance to negotiate a very high price.

Related Rules Nos. 33: Negotiation Preparation; 52: Liquidity Timing

Acquisition Success Results from the Efficacy of the Integration Plan

ACQUISITION VALUE, from the perspective of the purchaser, is determined by:

- Presence of a customized integration plan
- Merit and realism of the integration plan
- Execution of the integration plan

This idea is best illustrated by a comprehensive example—EMC Corp (NYSE: EMC), (*BusinessWeek*, "The Fine Art of Tech Mergers," (bibliography number 7). In 2002, CEO Joseph Tucci decided to embark on a diversification program to move the data storage hardware company into software. Over three years, EMC acquired seventeen companies, growing software to thirty-seven percent of its $9.6 billion in revenues. Many of the acquisitions have been small niche players with values under $100 million; some acquisitions have had barely $1 million in sales. The largest acquisition was Documentum for $1.7 billion.

EMC's process involves both science and art. The science consists of an integration team that creates customized integration plans for each deal. They create the plan from an integration "playbook" covering the pre-close period, the day of closing, and one hundred days thereafter. It covers transition procedures for leadership, business processes, computer systems, and sales. The acquisition is then closely tracked for six quarters to monitor progress.

The artistry, they say, is keeping the acquired employees productive and fully engaged. In that regard, fifteen of the seventeen acquired CEOs are still with the company. To transition the CEOs, each is assigned an executive mentor to help keep the CEO committed and involved.

There are, of course, many other issues and actions EMC evaluates to achieve its deal based ROI. EMC also believes in the power of learning from the unique aspects of each deal. While EMC may not be the best or only well-organized acquirer, it provides a very good example. The power of the process they exemplify is seen in the:

- Presence of a customized integration plan
- Human resources dedicated to the process
- Efforts to maintain CEO and management engagement
- Performance and human resource monitoring post-closing

These processes may also suggest important acquisition negotiating points (Rule No. 33).

Related Rule No. 33: Negotiation Preparation

Dealing With Entrepreneurs

FOR THIRD PARTIES TRYING TO DEAL SUCCESSFULLY with entrepreneurs, remember those salient characteristics of entrepreneurs that we talked about in Rule No. 2. Successful entrepreneurs:

- Have short attention spans
- Are single minded in achieving their objectives
- Seek control
- Possess a passionate belief in their company, its products, and themselves
- Are aggressively argumentative

The point of this discussion is to indicate, on the one hand, what to expect in discussions with entrepreneurs, and, on the other hand, what kinds of approaches will capture an entrepreneur's interest.

If you understand the characteristics listed above, you may find the following techniques useful:

- Get to the point quickly.
- Listen carefully for important nuances.
- Praise the entrepreneur's company, products, and accomplishments.
- Lay out alternatives, creating a feeling that the entrepreneur is in control.
- Remind the entrepreneur that his next best alternative involves considerable dilution, difficulty, and delay for his company (Rule No. 30).
- Focus on substance, and graciously ignore the entrepreneur's overselling and aggressive argument in response to proposals.
- Stress the great future potential of teamwork—i.e., what your company will do to increase market acceptance, etc.
- Provide strong financial incentives.

- Suggest a quick timeline for bringing the transaction to a conclusion.
- Plan to minimize entrepreneur's involvement in corporate bureaucracy.
- Follow-up frequently after closing (Rule No. 55).

Related Rule No. 2: Lead from Strengths; 30: Negotiation Posture; 55: Acquisition Success

Rule No. 57

In an Acquisition, an Entrepreneur's Effectiveness Lasts Twelve to Thirty-six Months

WHEN ENTREPRENEURS ARE ACQUIRED, the acquirers should have well-considered expectations and plans for them (Rules Nos. 55 and 56). As you consider and plan their continued usefulness, use the following guides:

- Clarify the duties and reporting structure early; do it at the time of the agreement in principle.
- Provide senior managers with strong incentives during this timeframe (Rule No. 55).
- Meddle in the operations of the acquisition as little as possible for the first six months after closing.
- For the first year, involve the entrepreneur and the entrepreneur's team in the parent company only occasionally.
- Plan for a phase-out of the entrepreneur over this time frame based on direct discussion with the entrepreneur and others working with him.

Mutual productivity results from a deliberate plan that provides considerable room for the entrepreneur to innovate with the fewest distractions. But at the same time, the plan will phase the entrepreneur out when his effectiveness or interest falls off (Rules Nos.2, 51 and 55).

Many acquirers have predetermined integration plans for acquisitions. Such programs probably do not work well for entrepreneurs. Young companies need custom-developed integration plans to maintain their passion, innovation, and momentum. Buyers should think in terms of three six-month periods. Compare this with EMC's process in Rule No. 55, suggesting custom-tailored integration time periods.

- The first six months is for essential items such as integration of the financial function and possibly the sales force.

- The second period is for integrating other functions that create operating cost savings and efficiencies.
- The third period is used to complete all planned areas of integration.

Large companies can easily overwhelm entrepreneurial companies during integration, and may inadvertently destroy the very asset that they bought. Consequently, a time phased approach is recommended and should be developed based on the specific facts and potential integration economics between the companies. The best time to reach mutual understanding on the integration plan is at the agreement in principle—not after the transaction is closed.

Related Rules: No. 2: Leading from Strength; No. 51: Pass the Baton; No. 55: Acquisition Success; No. 56: Dealing with Entrepreneurs

PART 5

EPILOGUE

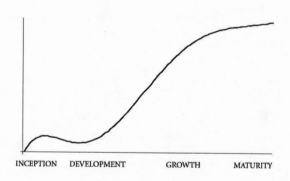

INCEPTION   DEVELOPMENT   GROWTH   MATURITY

Young Companies Are High Speed Roller Coasters

ENTREPRENEURS EXPERIENCE the highest highs and the lowest lows—sometimes in the same day. Events reverse themselves at such speeds that they can easily shred a person's psyche. The issues range across customers, products, technical programs, competitors, employees, and investors. To make matters worse, such things happen 24/7, so calls, meetings, and discussions often don't fit neatly into "normal business hours." Such events wreak havoc on family, friends, and subordinates, as well as on the entrepreneur.

The skill here is to develop coping mechanisms for these rapid swings to prevent leadership from breaking down. You are not ready for entrepreneurship until you can balance enough passionate involvement for business leadership with enough detachment to survive the death-dealing crosscurrents. Celebrate the real successes, but don't "manufacture" them.

As soon as a young company achieves annual revenue growth rates above about thirty-five percent, management is probably in a constant state of chaos. Corporate chaos is a consideration in the management selection process (Rule No. 11), information system design (Rule No. 27), and staff meetings (Rule No. 15).

If the entrepreneurial process proves too difficult, you have to look in a mirror and know that the mission and/or the person is wrong for this roller coaster ride.

Related Rules Nos. 11: Manager Selection; 15: Staff Meetings; 27: MIS

Rule No. 59

Nothing Succeeds Like Genuine Passion

AN ENTREPRENEUR'S EFFUSIVE PASSION for innovation, products, market disruption, technologies, and strategies is contagious and attracts good investors, top tier customers, and superior management.

But there are those unworthy leaders who bring a kind of false, seductive passion to the task. To understand the difference between the true and the false, one has only to compare Joan of Arc with Enron executives. One may look at leading companies such as Google, Starbucks, and Cisco to see how genuine passion permeates organizations.

Losing the passion, conversely, means it's time to either change the mission or to exit the venture.

BIBLIOGRAPHY

1. Augustine, Norman, *Augustine's Laws*, Restin, VA, AIAA, 1997.
2. "Become Innovators-in-Chief," April 24, 2006, *BusinessWeek*, pages 68-70.
3. Bounds, Gwendolyn, May 23, 2006, "More Than Squeaking By," *Wall Street Journal*, pages B1, 4.
4. Etter, Lauren, May 20, 2006, "Enron Waiting for a Verdict," *Wall Street Journal*, page A7.
5. Farrell, Greg, July 31, 2006, "Business Plans Should Be Simple, Passionate," *USA Today*, page 5E.
6. Foust, Dean, May 29, 2006, "Tough Love at the Office" (review of *The Managerial Moment of Truth*) *BusinessWeek*, Page 106.
7. Hamm, Steve, July 10, 2006, "The Fine Art of Tech Mergers," *BusinessWeek*, pages 70-72.
8. King, W.J., *The Unwritten Laws Of Engineering*, NYC, NY, Acme Press, 2001.
9. Krikland, Rik, July 10, 2006, "The Real CEO Pay Problem," *Fortune*, pages 78-84.
10. Leonhardt, David, May 3, 2006, "Rule No. 35: Reread Rule On Integrity," *New York Times*, pages C1, 7.
11. Lucchetti, Aaron, August 24, 2006, "A Verdict on Grasso's Legacy," *Wall Street Journal*, pages C1, 4.
12. Nocera, Joe, May 27, 2006, "The Board Wore Chicken Suits," *New York Times*, pages B1, 9.
13. Pimentel, Benjamin, September 10, 2006, "HP Chair Sitting on a Hot Seat," *San Francisco Chronicle*, pages F1, 5.
14. "Quattrone Could Get $120 Million Payout," August 24, 2006, *San Francisco Chronicle*, pages C1, 2.
15. Said, Carolyn, May 26, 2006, "From White Collars to Prison Blues," *San Francisco Chronicle*, pages D1, 6.

16. Sorkin, Andrew, August 19, 2006, "Tech Banker Avoids Third Trial," *San Francisco Chronicle,* pages C1, 2.

17. Tonyareiman.com-information on body language.

18. Welch, Jack, January 29, 2007, "Hiring Wrong-and Right," *BusinessWeek, page 102.*

19. Welch, Jack, May 8, 2006, "How Healthy Is Your Company?" *BusinessWeek,* page 126.

20. Welch, Jack, June 26, 2006, "Stop the B.S. Budgets," *BusinessWeek,* page 114.

George Von Gehr is a proven counselor to entrepreneurs and their advisors. He had front-line experience as an entrepreneur before starting, growing, and selling his successful boutique technology investment banking firm. His background includes degrees in engineering, law and business from Princeton and Stanford as well as consulting with McKinsey & Company, Inc. An avid car enthusiast and collector, he lives with his wife in Pebble Beach, California and San Juan Island, Washington.

978-0-595-41854-1
0-595-41854-6